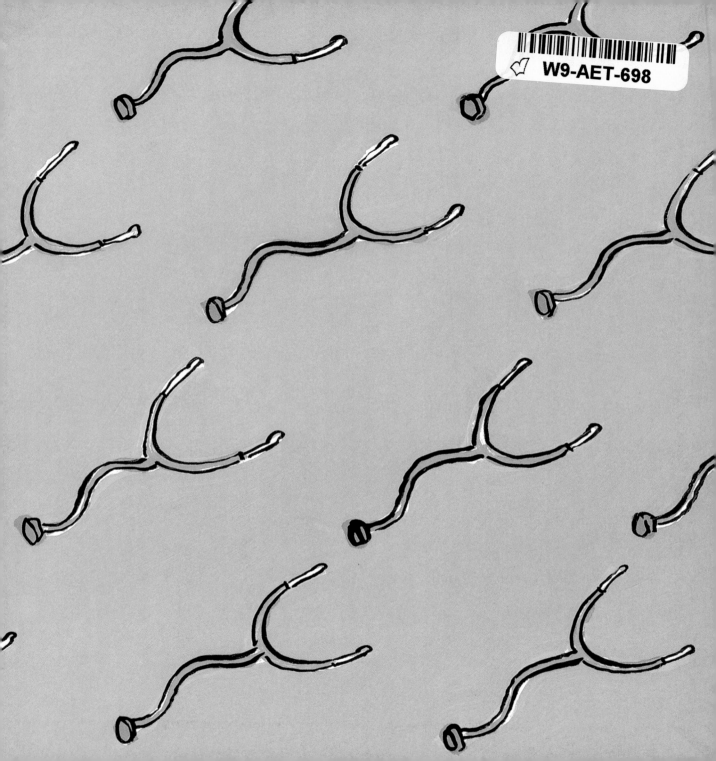

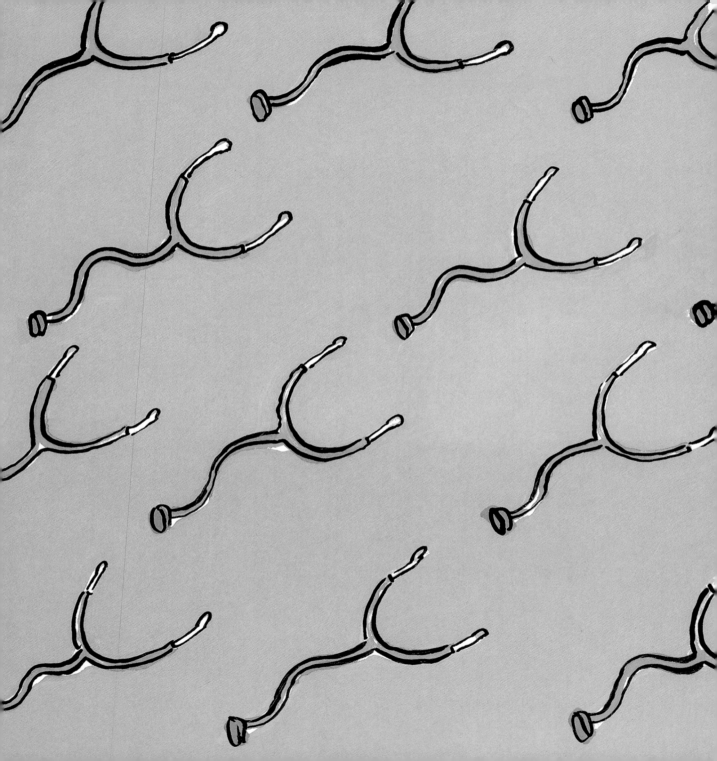

Dear Parents,

Children's earliest experiences with stories and books usually involve grown-ups reading to them. However, reading should be active, and as adults, we can help young readers make meaning of the text by prompting them to relate the book to what they already know and to their personal experiences. Our questions will lead them to move beyond the simple story and pictures and encourage them to think beneath the surface. For example, after reading a story about the sleep habits of animals, you might ask, "Do you remember when you moved into a big bed? Could you see the moon out of your window?"

Illustrations in these books are wonderful and can be used in a variety of ways. Your questions about them can direct the child to details and encourage him or her to think about what those details tell us about the story. You might ask the child to find three different "beds" used by animals and insects in the book. Illustrations can even be used to inspire readers to draw their own pictures related to the text.

At the end of each book, there are some suggested questions and activities related to the story. These questions range in difficulty and will help you move young readers from the text itself to thinking skills such as comparing and contrasting, predicting, applying what they learned to new situations and identifying things they want to find out more about. This conversation about their reading may even result in the children becoming the storytellers, rather than simply the listeners!

Harriet Ziefert, M.A.
Language Arts/Reading Specialist

More to Think About

Does a Bear Wear Boots?

Does a Beaver Sleep in a Bed?

Does a Camel Cook Spaghetti?

Does an Owl Wear Eyeglasses?

Does a Panda Go to School?

Does a Seal Smile?

Does a Tiger Go to the Dentist?

Does a Woodpecker Use a Hammer?

Think 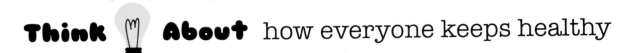 About how everyone keeps healthy

Does a Hippo Go to the Doctor?

Harriet Ziefert • illustrations by **Emily Bolam**

BLUE APPLE

Text copyright © 2006, 2014 by Harriet Ziefert
Illustrations copyright © 2006 by Emily Bolam
CIP data is available.
Published in the United States 2014 by
 Blue Apple Books
515 Valley Street, Maplewood, NJ 07040
www.blueapplebooks.com
Printed in China
ISBN: 978-1-60905-450-2
1 3 5 7 9 10 8 6 4 2
07/14

Does a hippo go to the doctor?

Oh, no!

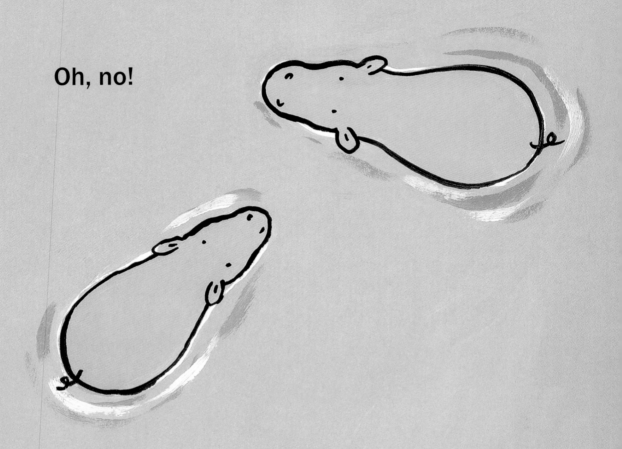

**A hippopotamus does
not go to the doctor.**

Does a zebra go to the doctor?

A zebra grazes in the wild.
The doctor would have a hard time listening to
its heart and lungs with a stethoscope.

Does a rhinoceros go to the doctor?

Hippos and zebras and rhinos
are all wild animals. They cannot easily
be examined by doctors.

Dogs and cats are domestic animals,
and they can be examined by doctors.
Animal doctors are called veterinarians.

Farm animals—horses, cows, goats, and sheep—
are also treated by veterinarians.

Vets also treat large animals
when they live in zoos.

Any sick animal can be dangerous, so the doctors who take care of them are very careful.

The doctor who takes care of you is also careful...
careful to keep her hands clean and
her instruments sterile.

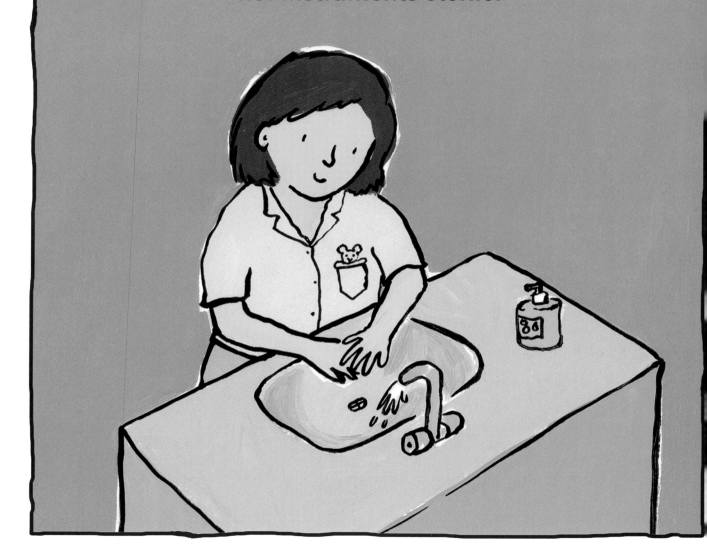

Look at the tongue depressor.
The doctor uses it to check Joey's
mouth and throat, then puts
it into a special trash bin.

What's this?

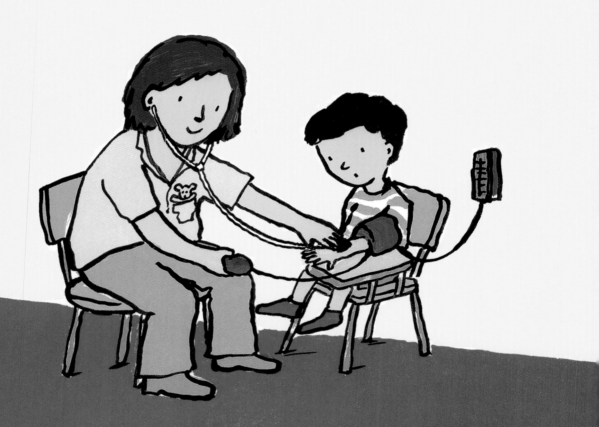

It's a sphygmomanometer, or
blood pressure cuff. The doctor uses
it to check Alex's blood pressure.

What's this?

It's a special scale for babies.

The nurse uses it to weigh Alex's sister, then she'll use a tape measure to see how long the baby is from the top of her head to the tip of her toes.

What's this?

It's a syringe.
The doctor uses it to give Rosie an injection.
She is careful to keep everything sterile and
tries not to hurt. But there is a prick and a pinch.
Rosie says, "Ouch!"

Then Rosie gets to choose a bandage.

Rosie is not afraid to go to the doctor. She knows what's going to happen at the doctor's office. And she knows she'll get a surprise when she's done.

Which stickers would you like?

Dr. Debbie says you should have a checkup
every year to keep track of:

- how much you have grown
- how much you weigh
- whether your bones are growing straight
- whether you have received all the shots you need
- whether there are any problems with your hearing
- whether there are any problems with your eyes
- whether your heart and lungs and kidneys are working
  the way they should

Now it's time for a checkup for Rosie's doll.

Thank you, Rosie!

Think 💡 About how everyone keeps healthy

This book compares wild animals, who don't go to doctors, to pets, who go to vets. It then looks at people, who go to different kinds of doctors for checkups and when they are sick.

Compare and Contrast

Compare a sick zebra and a sick horse.

• Who takes care of them? Why is it different?

Many veterinarians take care of both cats and dogs.

• How do cats and dogs get to the vet? How do they act when they get there?

• How does an elephant get a shot? How do you get a shot?

• How are they different and the same?

Research

Go to a library or online and find out what different doctors do:

• pediatrician

• orthopedist

• cardiologist

• allergist

• ophthalmologist

• psychiatrist

• surgeon

Find out how a veterinarian keeps a dog, or a cat, or a bunny healthy.

• What shots? What medicines? What vitamins?

Next time you are at the doctor's office, look around.

• Ask the doctor or nurse what the different tools are used for.

Write a list of things you would like to know about the body.

• Check a book out of the library on how bodies work to look up answers.

Observe

Make a chart.

- Record your weight and height every month.

Watch someone with a cold.

- What symptoms does he or she have, and how does he or she treat them?

Observe your family's daily routine.

- What do they do to stay healthy?

Write, Tell, or Draw

Write a story in which you are the doctor and your friend is the patient.

- What if your sister or brother is the patient?

Draw a picture of yourself at the doctor.

- Is your face curious? Worried? Both?

Write or tell a story about yourself as a veterinarian in your neighborhood or at a zoo.